Angel Fingerprints

The Little Book of Joyous Thoughts

ANGEL FINGERPRINTS
The Little Book of Joyous Thoughts

By Sharon Warren   Art by Elsie Petrequin-Noble
Copyright © 1995 by Sharon Warren. All Rights Reserved.
Title inspired by a quote from Carlos Santana, NBC, Oct. 1994
Published by:
Sourcebooks, Inc., P.O. Box 4410, Naperville, Illinois 60567-4410
(630) 961-3900 FAX: (630) 961-2168
ISBN: 1-57071-445-2
Library of Congress Catalog Card Number 94-96699
1. Epigrams 2. Life - Quotations, maxims, etc. 3. Love - Quotations, maxims, etc.
I. Petrequin-Noble, Elsie. II. Title.
PN1441.W37.A54 1995   94-96699
808'.882-dc20
Printed in THE UNITED STATES OF AMERICA
EB 10 9 8 7 6 5

ANGEL FINGERPRINTS
The Little Book of Joyous Thoughts
by Sharon Warren

Cover design by Elsie Petrequin-Noble
Art & Calligraphy by Elsie Petrequin-Noble

Other books by Sharon Warren
& Elsie Petrequin-Noble

ONE LIGHT ONE LOVE
LONG LONG AGO

Music CD by Michael McCabe & Sharon Warren
ONE LIGHT ONE LOVE, Vol. I

For information call: (888) 493-7310

*"All of us carry a lot of pain. Healing means to be whole and sound…that's my job…I work with sound…so we heal people. I believe in my heart that Angels today…what they long for the most is for us to have more compassion. When you do something for the Highest Good for all people, those are the **fingerprints that Angels leave behind.**"*

quote by Carlos Santana

ANGELS II: Beyond The Light, NBC - Oct. 1994

Special thanks to Keith Johannessen, whose faith
and love inspired and created these
precious thoughts that we now share with you.
To my dear mother, Thelma Gay Smith,
who has loved me always.
To Elsie Petrequin-Noble,
whose artistry transforms hearts and lives.
To Carol Guthrie Sjolander, Cheryl Long Riffle,
Steve Vaile, LaVon Richards, Colette DeWitt,
Janet Holbrook and all the friends who believe
in our vision of this little book of joyous thoughts.
Heartfelt appreciation to Paul Clemens.

To my brothers
John, Gerald, and Howard Jr.

In loving memory of my father
Howard A. Smith

I will find happiness when I give to others
what I most want for myself...
Love, acceptance, peace, tolerance, and freedom

God is my center
I accept what is
I am Love

A heart that is truly open gives Love to all
and receives Love from all

Trust…love…be strong and independent
Give all the Love you feel in your heart
That is your reward…to give Love

Let the heavens dance between us
for that is the silence which allows
the notes of our song
to be heard

God is
I am
Let go
So it is

Nothing on this earthly plane can separate
what God has joined together in LOVE

I savor the memories of yesterday
and live in the now of my existence

True, pure, unconditional Love never dies

Let me hold you in my heart, my soul,
and in my dreams…
experiencing you in my mind…for loving you
has given me the power to know who I really am

Safely surrounded by the peace of Love,
I drift in a sea of warm, velvet sounds
of a summer breeze

Great Spirit, grant that our hearts
may always be young
and our dreams may last forever

Trust

Beyond forever we have come
Forever Home we fly

As I wait in the silence of my heart,
my Love shines like a beacon in the night

You are all Light
and all Love and all embracing
You create all

Love sustains us
on life's turbulent waters

You are wonderful!
You bring out the best in people,
and they bring out the best in you

The energy is flowing
You bring me so much joy

Talk with me
Laugh with me
Play with me
Be with me
Be like a child with me

Light

The moon that you gaze upon
shines down on me

You are a little girl in a beautiful flower garden
There are no spiders in your garden

You are gold
You are shining
You are brilliant

You are becoming a diamond!
A beautiful, clear,
light-gathering and reflective,
multi-faceted person,
full of fire and brilliance

I cannot imagine
Heaven being more beautiful
Than this very moment
As my being fills
With the essence of you

You are beautiful
You are loved

Together two hearts beat as one…
Born of Love, Eternal Love

You are a diamond…I am one, too
Facet-nating and brilliant

I am not leaving you
I am with you always
My heart is with you

Stay connected

Love is the doorway
Love is the key
Love is the bridge
Between you and me

Sail on through the storm
though the journey be long

Delight in being human
For there we find lessons in life
and appreciation for living

Trust in Divine Order…Let go…Relax…
Everything is fine…
Perfect

In the center of the storm is the calm
Move with the storm…have faith
and let go of those things you can't control

Only the illusion of time and space
separates our two hearts

Rise toward the Light…
We have lessons to learn

Each moment is a MIRACLE!
Embrace the miracle
and the wonder of life

In Love I have Power
In Power there is endless Love

Don't be perfect…Forgive yourself!

Serenity, focus…
Be calm and enjoy the wonder

What is magical shall never pass away
Be your own magician
Create your illusions to then…
Make your own reality

A woman's worth is infinite
A man's worth is boundless

I create fulfilling magical relationships…
where imagination, together with illusion,
instill real feelings of intimacy

ELEVEN means we stand independent
as individuals,
yet together, side by side, a greater Power
than the sum of two

I do not own you
I do not possess you
Therefore, I cannot lose you

I'm glad it didn't take a lifetime
to find you again

I celebrate the beautiful you
that you are becoming…
a butterfly emerging from the darkness…
a Phoenix rising from the ashes

I love every nuance of you

I see the precious you
that you have always been

Your life is a gift
you share with the world,
and my life is richer
because I have known you

Our spirits fly so high
Each day of life is a miracle
We are One Light One Love

May you walk in the Light
knowing you are loved

May you feel the magnificence of the
Power and the Love that you are

I am with you
In that place
Where time
And space
Don't exist
We are Love

When two people share the same dreams
those dreams come true

When making Love becomes a sacrament…
a testimony to the Glory of God,
we are in Heaven

My heart is your home,
and my spirit plays in your garden

Only Love is real…our relationship
exists to serve Spirit

I am real
I am in you
And in your imagination
You are in me
And in my imagination

Join with the fear
See Oneness in all
Rise out of the flames
From the ashes below

I believe in you
My heart is with you
Know I am with you always

I Love to touch you
I touch to Love you

Life can be magic
Life can be tragic
What are you going
to make of it?

You hold the key to the doors
of all your dreams

The Soul speaks
through eyes of Love

Take my hand
Walk beside me
Toward the Light
Beyond the sun

With all Creation, we are One

Walk on Love's light-strewn path
Safe and warm…evermore

In our minds…in our hearts…Love is fulfilled
We are One

Thank you for the smile in your voice
Thank you for the truth on your lips
Thank you for the Love in your Soul

I see your form, your flaws, your fears…
I still Love you

Thank you for the peace in your touch
Thank you for the desire in your breath
Thank you for the Light in your heart

I know your strengths, your weaknesses, too…
and I Love you

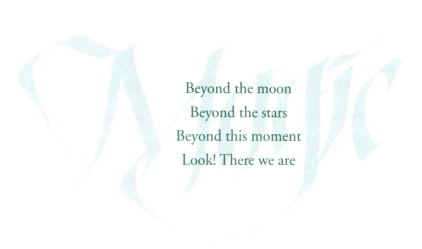

Beyond the moon
Beyond the stars
Beyond this moment
Look! There we are

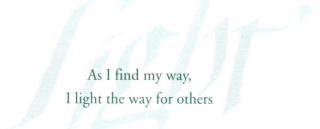

As I find my way,
I light the way for others

Love waits there where hearts are free

Magical, mystical, miracle…LOVE

Web of Life
Catch my dreams
See them grow
My heart is Light
It now has wings

The Truth of Love…it never fails,
though wander far we may

Listen with your heart…not your mind,
your emotions, your body, your ears, your eyes

We've come so far from who we were
to who we are today

Your Love has come
to heal my lonely heart

Harness your sexual energy…
direct it toward creative efforts
and you will change the world

Love is a flower…
rejoice in the unfolding

The sound of your voice touches my ears like
Angels' voices speaking to my heart

Peace

May we rest our wings
beside the still waters of Love…
Home again